HORIZONS
THE BEGINNING
AND THE END

HORIZONS THE BEGINNING AND THE END

By

Franklin V. McQueen

Published by Wiley-DeRamus Publishing
6220-F Elgywood Lane
Charlotte, North Carolina 28213

1stBooks - rev. 11/13/00

Progress is measured through
Struggle and continuity
Reward is gained through
Patience and endurance

ACKNOWLEDGEMENTS

All praises to God (Allah, Jah, Jehovah) from whom all blessings flow. Mrs. E.J. David, my 10th grade biology teacher, who assisted me in continuing my college education. Dr. Redmon, my writing instructor, and Benedict College. My closest friends, Jannise Manning and family; James Jacobs and family; Lavernia David and family; include Ben Johnson and Edith Bridges. My God-daughters, Angelica and Alexis. Mrs. Helen Hayes and her timeless typing; Mrs. Connie Wiley-DeRamus and Mr. Larry Sith for their valuable assistance, the Gamma Pi Chapter and all the guys who gathered around the pot and all others who shared fond memories. "Asante" (thanks). Love, Peace. Also Myra Cunningham and Richard Noble and Aundrey Sutton for his photo addition.

DEDICATION

I dedicate this book to my immediate family: my parents, brothers, sisters, nephews and nieces. And to my extended family: the McQueens, the Richardson, the Pounceys, the Williamses and the Croslands.

Special dedication to Leroy and Billy Pouncey, Thomas McRae, Wilbert Boatwright, and Anna Pouncey.

TABLE OF CONTENTS

JOURNEYING

Endowed by the Creater to be
All that I can be.
To find all that's within me.
Confronted by adversity.
I will always be me.

INTRODUCTION

This collection of my most cherished possessions encompasses years of labor, deliberation and dedication. Because of my experiences, whether triumphs or failures, I have decided to share with you my thoughts, feelings, emotions and expectations. Hope you enjoy.

WHO AM I? AND WHERE AM I GOING?

Who am I? Where am I going?
I am a man of substance, born in this
World of mysticism.
I have been given five senses, with which
I am able to gather, analyze and resolve
The things of the unknown.
In such a complex world, maybe one day I
Will find myself.
As for where I am going, that is not clear,
But I have set many goals in life;
The most important is to write what I
Consider to be my masterpiece in which its
Substance will be of such significance that
The world will be able to relate.

MY WALK

I walk a mile and many miles,
But, I always do it with a smile.
One may look at another and
say, why does he walk from day to day?
For I have a long road ahead
And I shall travel it until I'm dead,
And if I should stumble and fall, it
would have been worth it all.

MY TALK

Yesterday, I came upon a little
girl crying. When she saw me
she turned her head. I told her
that I didn't mind because
everyone cries from time to time.
And after I had talked with her for
A while, I felt good inside because
I left her with a smile.

WHY NOT?

Like any other man I have a dream,
I dream of being something someday, Some say
there'll never be, but so say this is not for me.

Because I think I can fulfill my
dreams and because it's mine, I still
dream this dream until the end of my time.

Some say good things come to those
that wait, and I dream of one day of
becoming something great.

HEAVEN

They tell me of a land that's far, far
Away. A land that everyone wants to go
One day. It's land that money can't
Buy, no matter how hard you try.

It's a land of love and peace, and many
Beautiful things to see. You'll go there
If you live in the right way. No matter
What people might say.

THE PRAYER

Lord! What's happening to this world.
I see and hear things ever day, why
Must it be this way?

In my land we hear of inflation, but in
Others we hear of starvation.
Lord! How much longer must those people
Live in hunger!

Lord! We are living in a crucial time.
I can't put it aside, it stays on my mind. Lord!
I'm on my knees to pray, that tomorrow will be a better day.

YESTERDAY

Yesterday I had a dream
I recall how wonderful it seemed.
There was no pollution, the air was clean.

Yesterday I dreamed that all wars had ceased.
Everyone lived in love and peace.

Yesterday I had a dream that the world was
free of hatred and sin.
Everyone was working together.
No one had to contend with each other.

Yesterday I dreamed a wonderful dream, but
I awoke to discover that it was only fantasy.
Nothing had changed, this old world was still
the same.

LOVE

We've got to have love, love for our God
above. We've got to have peace, peace
We must pray for all wars to cease.
We've got to have joy, joy we must come
together, we must not destroy.
We must all come hand in hand, not only
here, but clear across the land. How long
does it take for us to learn? That men are
men, the only difference is the color of our skin.
Why must we fight? Don't we know that
It's not right? How many more years?
How many more tears?

CONFUSION

Looking out my window, bewildered by the
things of life and what lies in store for me.

I often dream of things the way I wish them
to be. My mind filled with many illusions
never coming to any conclusions.

MY FRIENDS

Where are my friends?
Where have they gone?
They all have seemed to
have left me alone.
Where are my friends?
What have they done?
I am speaking of all,
not just one.
It would be alright if
I could see them every
now and then, but it
seems as though I will
never see them again.
Where are my friends?
I hope they are fine,
for I shall think about
them until the end of my
time.

LOST CHILD

I am a lost child, I have no mother,
father, sister, or brother, I have no
home to call my own, no bed to rest my
head.
I ramble about from day to day,
and at night I find an alley in which
to stay. Yesterday I asked a man of a
different color for a dime. He wouldn't
give it because I wasn't his kind.
I told him that it's not the color
of my skin, that it is what's within.
I said that regardless of my color, "Help
Me", for I am still his brother.

DESTINY

I looked into the sky
Saw a condensed light
I began to run
I fled in fright
I looked back and I could
see this condensed light
coming after me.
And I screamed, oh God!
What can it be?
Is the world coming to an end?
From where I've come, it must
now return.
I fell to my knees and began
to pray, for I could no longer
see my way.
I began to scream, I began to
holler, for there was no
direction I could follow;
And I heard a voice saying
it's your end.
I looked, I saw, and I said,
Amen.

BROKEN HOME

I pray nightly, that the fussing
And fighting would cease. But,
Now I know it will never. And
Now that it's over, I wonder if
It's wrong. Because we now
Have a broken home.

THE CHILDREN

Morning comes
A child is born,
Pray for the children.
When darkness comes
And there is no light to
Be seen,
Pray for the children.
They need your guidance.
They need your helping hand.
Pray for the children
When morning comes and I'm
Here no longer hear,
Don't shed a tear,
Just pray for the children.

TOMORROW'S CHILDREN

Pictures of the past
Times I thought would forever last.
Me and my friends playing in the sand,
making all sorts of plans dreaming
Days we thought would never end as children
But the years began to grow, those days
are no more times are changing
But, there are cherished memories of joy and
laughter
Places we used to gather as children
And in regret, we say good-bye, sometimes
as we look back and cry in sorrow,
For some have passed on, but for us survivors,
We must carry on for Tomorrow's Children

MOTHER

There is a special woman in my life
Who is neither my mistress or my wife.
When I was an infant, Mother lay me on her
Breast, whenever she thought I needed rest.
When I needed help, she was always there, with
warm and gentle loving care.
This woman, my mother, I shall forever lover her.

HOME

I left home this morning
Lord! I hated to go.
Where I was going,
Lord! I didn't know.
Mother was weeping,
Lord! She was crying.
To see her that way
God, I felt like dying.
Father was hurt, but he
kept his pride,
He only shook my hand and
said, may God be by your side.
My brother who was older,
walked over and put his
hand on my shoulder.
Said for me to do what's
right, to pray and put
trust in God and everything
would be alright.
And as I turned to see my
other sisters, siblings, their eyes
filled with tears. I walked over
and kissed them all good-bye and
for them not to cry.
And when I was to enter the car
I heard my mother's voice saying,
son, don't forget to write.
And my brother's say, brother take
it light.
But one day when I've found the
answer to my dream, I'm going
home where the trees grow tall
Home! to my family, for Lord I love
them all.

BLACK WOMAN

Black Woman
Robbed of your virtue
Taken away from your man
But somehow he has been able to withstand
Black Woman
Taken away from your child
While all the while you cried and moaned
In the face of degredation
You kept right on
You are strong, so be proud
Stand with dignity.
Black woman
The time is here, the season, the year
Take off the mask, stop living in that unreal world
My queen, my brother's Queen
If you portray yourself in such a way.
Black Woman.
I only think that it is time you be what is truly you
Be a real Queen
I am proud of you.
Black Woman
I write these words in the hope that you will better
understand, and help my brother to understand that our
ancestors didn't dream a dream to go dead.

THERE'S NO PLACE LIKE HOME

Mother, I'm coming home,
I never told you but I was alone.
Mother, I've committed a crime.
And now I have served my time.

Wherein I was once strong,
But now I am weak,
because there were times
I couldn't eat or sleep.
I would lay in my cell from day to day
Never having anything to say.

I know you've wondered where I've been
I spared you shame, I've paid for my sin.
Mother, I write these words in tears
I'm coming home, I'm lonely, it's been a
lot of years.

Mother, with God's help
I'm coming home
I will no longer be alone.

SOMEDAY

We laughed
We talked
and I adored the smile
upon your face
You are my friend
Now -
and forever more
And wherever the winds may take me
there will always be
the thought of you -
You're kind, you care
You are my friend
this song is for you
I wish you happiness your whole life through -
Memories that will never die
Feelings felt so deeply that in the midst of
my sorrow,
I the man who didn't want to cry,
I would weep in my sleep.
Now I relinquish the love I most
desired to give,
But, someday, underneath the misty blue skies,
Somewhere beyond the horizon,
I'll find happiness.

TO ME

To me you are like a beautiful flower.
Enjoying the freshness of a spring shower.
Giving love from hour to hour.

To me you're one of a kind
You're black, beautiful and superfine.
A girl like you is every man's dream,
At least to me that's the way it seems.

I have so little – so much to gain –
Still I wish you were mine the same
Wherever I go, no matter where
You'll always be in my daily prayer.

WELCOME HOME

I was sitting home so sadly, and blue.
When all of a sudden I heard a knock at
the door. And when I opened it, there stood you.
My heart took a thump and then another.
It seemed as though I was about to smother.
There I stood not able to speak
Because just seeing you standing there
made me weak. I was in agony all the
months that had passed.
And now you're home at last. After a while
I said, come on in baby, come on home,
Because this is where you belong.
No more lonely nights, no more tears to shed.
Everything is going to be alright.
At last I have you back home to make love to,
to whisper in your ear, Baby, I love you,
and to hear you say, I love you.
But most of all, to have you home
And with you, there is no wrong.

ANGENETTA

There's a girl whose name is Angenetta
I would like to get to know her better
But to do this is hard for me
Because she is a girl I seldom see,
This girl, she's my kind, because
No man can seem to blow her mind
But I shall do what no man has done
Just give me a little time.
This girl is like the most beautiful
Things that grow
And they are flowers and she's most like
The rose that's fresh and pure
She could make anyone feel secure.
People like her make the world worthwhile
Not only by what she says or does
But sometimes in her smile.

LOVE ME

I heard the sound of your voice
calling my name
Blowing in the wind
Girl, this love I kept locked inside
I offer it to you
Please take it
Because love was made to give away
and I give my love to you
I love you
Please take it
All the days I live life alone
Sadly would my heart sing
and I wished for the touch of you
I love you
come spread this joy around the world
There's so much to give
My heart is so full of love for you
Please take it
I offer it to you.

MEN OF WAR

They lie on the ground a thousand times a thousand,
They lie on each other's blood, water and mud.
Never having a chance to think of love.
They have to fight to survive, and keep alive
they must strive.
Some must kill against their will, but in order
to stay alive, it's a must to kill.
All around them lie the dead, but they stay
there, and the battlefield is their bed.
And as they look around and see their friends
fall, they wonder if it's worth it all.
Sometimes they wonder about their loved ones
back home, and they long to be there.
And as they live through one day after the other
they wonder if they'll see another.
And after all the fighting and killing they may
lose their battle.
After that, nothing seems to matter, and everything
they fought for seems to shatter. Boom!

HE HAD A DREAM

He fought for racial equality,
And all that he had done, he did it
for you and me.

He was against violence because wherein
Others would take to fighting, he kept
His silence. Sometimes there were threats
Against his life, children and wife.
No matter how many threats there were, he
Went on, because he knew God had given him
A mission. And for him to quit, it would
Have been wrong.

He has marched many a mile, with many by
His side, and no matter how many miles
There were, he went on wherein others would
take a ride.

Sometimes he was bruised and scared, and
His way seemed hard. But he knew he had to go
On until the problems were solved.

He believed that we could all live in love and
Peace, if we only tried. And he believed this
Until the day he died.
This man was Dr. Rev. Martin Luther King, Jr.
And all of you, no matter what your color may be,
What this man fought and died for, let it not
Be in vain.

THE WAY TO REMEMBER ME

If you never get a chance, this is the way I
want you all to remember me.

Not for what I am,
but rather what I want to be.

Not for what I've done,
but for what I want to do.

Not for what I said, but for what I wanted
to say. And pray for the chance one day.

WE MUST CONTINUE TO FIGHT

We were brought here
In balls and chains
Beaten and oppressed
We were put through the test
The test of torture
To be made ignorant;
Ignorant of our native land;
Ignorant of our native tongue;
Ignorant of our heritage;
But we bore the burden,
We beat the ship,
We did it with our mothers, fathers,
grandmothers, grandfathers,
great-grandmothers, great-grandfathers,
Blood, sweat, and tears
We made it through the most painful years.
We did it with hope, faith and determination.
We were determined to be free
To enjoy this world that God has made for all.
We have fought the battle of yesterday,
and we won.

But the war goes on
We must continue to fight,
As long as we have life,
We must continue to fight,
But let it be with honor, dignity, and pride.
Let words be your weapon,
Let words be your enemies' defeat;
Let words fight as long as words can.
But when words will no longer do,
Do what you have to do,
Be brave, bold and strong.

ACHIEVE

Crawl, little baby, crawl
Run free.
Learn, little baby, learn
Store what you see.
Because as days grow into
months, weeks and years,
The greater become your
Want joyful tears
Because all that you can
Hear, feel, smell, touch,
And see
Will be, will change
Darkness into day
Summer sun into cold wintry winds
Failure into victory
Anything you want in life
There it is

Achieve.

DARK END OF THE STREET

A place locked in time,
Visions in my mind,
At the dark end of the street.
Children playing merrily,
Rhythm and rhymes at the dark
end of the street.

Once where light shone so bright,
on a moonlit night,
Voices at the dark end of the street.

There was Joseph and James
Perry and Mary, Gwen and Charles,
And Jannise and many others
at the dark end of the street.

A place locked in time,
Visions in my mind
at the dark end of the street.

GRANDMA

I remember Grandma's kitchen
Her standing there washing dishes
as she hummed.
She would sometimes sing out loud,
a song or two before she was through.
I remember her gentle ways,
My! How I remember those days.
Grandma lending a helping hand
to a boy trying to become a man,
in a world he could not understand.
I remember the day Grandma went away,
Mamma called us all from play to say,
goodbye.
While we asked the questions, why?
A loss our hearts could feel, our
Eyes filled with tears.
I often visit the place of memories
full of fun in the big yard where we
played.
I know Grandma lives in heaven
her memory will be with me forever.

LOVE POEM

Last night somewhere in my sleep
There were visions of you in my mind
walking, holding hands on a warm summer day
it was wonderful!

Oh! The smile upon you face warmed my heart
through and through
and beats of sweet melody expressing I love you.

I love your touch, your gentle touch.
It soothes me so much.
And all the bad things that happen in life
Seem to go away.

I love the sparkles in your eyes.
They seem to say you're the only one in the world.
I love you boy, and oh, how I love you girl.

Morning came, and the visions slowly faded away.
Maybe today?

THE BUM

His life was spent mostly on street corners.
A bum, suggested by many that observed him.
Mr. Morrison - The Old Bum.
The children had heard their parents say this
time and time again. Mr. Morrison, the bum,
He always returned a warm smile.
For years this persisted until the old man
had become the talk of the town.
The bum who sat on the corner with
perceived disgusting manner.
Not that he ever did or said anything wrong to anyone.
He just sat on the corner, until one day
he lost his life saving the life of a child.

PLATEAU

Encouraged by the thought of tomorrow
depressed somewhat
Of the direction I should follow. But yet,
I shall forge with all the determination
That's within me to be the best that I can be.
The top of the mountain is mine.
Getting ready to get started again, I can, I will.
Once before, more next time.

THEME: LIFT HIM UP
"TO WHOM WHO IS A GIVER OF LIFE"

Who has bestowed upon man
dominion and authority upon the earth,
All praises to His name.
He who is the Epitome of beauty and benevolence,
The author of the world and all its inhabitants,
All praises to his name.
He is the giver of light,
The all wise and ever understanding entity
To whom we pray and trust for all our needs.
Sing Hallelujah!!!
He is the Way, the Truth, and the Light
In His path we should all follow.
In time of trouble, He will be your friend
And in His truth we can depend.
In His name we should be thankful
For the mountains and the valleys
The sunshine and the rain.
For life, health and strength.
He is the essence of knowledge,
The giver of hope.
To Him we should direct our faith.
THOU GOD! LIFT HIM UP!

NOT YET

Those were the years in looking back
I thought I would never get ahead.
Times were tough.
The days long and hard.
And the money never enough.
The endless hours of working the fields
in hope that providence would provide another meal.
Things were bad enough
Then there were the hopes and prayers
For tomorrow - a little flour or sugar
One might borrow
Sometimes I would imagine my world
All around me, riches - not rags until reality
Would descend at last
Back to a place aligned with hate
Men who would always be boys
Women who would always be gals
Boys and girls who would never grow up
the children of their parent,
slaves of their masters.
When freedom was an illusion
When the pain of the Negro man was the White man's laughter
It would be grand if we could only forget,
But not yet.

THOUGHTS

The creation of things to come
Infinite as the uncertain
Silhouette of life.

MIXED POEM

If you have a dream
dream your dream
and if you have a star
reach, no matter how far it
may seem.

Sometimes when we lose our loved
ones, we feel that we can't go on.
Because deep within as we feel
that a part of us is gone.
Soon we realize, this world keeps turning.
Life goes on.
We come to understand death!
God has put into His plan.

TRIBUTE TO MOTHER

Down through the years, I have observed you with
intense and passionate awareness.
I have been amazed at your sense of will
and determination.
You have, in calculated
and calibrated measures,
demonstrated the acts of diplomacy
and decision-making
in my lonely hours of despair and
bewilderment,
you have been a shining and reverent light of
motivation and inspiration. Your love and devotion
have been like soothing showers of spring,
blossoming beauty of flowers in the dawning light of hope,
In the tender moments of affection, you made
my heart glow with increasing joy and delight
knowing your strength has made me stronger.
Though time and distance sometimes have taken us apart,
the affection I feel for you will always be in my heart.
For you, Mother.

FATHER

Father of yesterday, today and tomorrow,
The meaning is the same.
You are a leader – a provider.
Your children shall call upon your name – Father.
Show me the way to a better day.
Guide me through the path of righteousness.
Encourage me to be my best – Father.
Love me so that I may know how to love.
Teach me the ways of the Almighty,
Father who art in Heaven. Teach me in the day
of my youth so that I will understand what is
required of me in a world so confusing.
Father – make our home a peaceful place,
filled with loving and joyful remembrance.

RIDE WITH FAITH

Crowned in my heart of discontent
Are the misery of people of all colors all nations.

The oppressed and the oppressor alike,
Both enslaved. The oppressed for want
of liberty. The oppressor, the misguided
illusions and bigotry. Such says
life. Such is history. All has its brief
moments of longevity. None has been infinite.

FALLING IN LOVE

Once upon a midnight sky
A star fell
A wish was made
A dream came true –
I met, fell in love,
And married you.

GREATNESS

The daring courageous – The patient –
The endurer – The sufferer –
The faithful – The worker – The
knowledgeable – The wise, and
The understanding.

A BLESSED AND CHERISHED MEMORY

The morning of December 21, 1949 was cold and rainy in the rural community of Marlboro County, several miles away from its capital of Bennettsville, South Carolina. The weather forecast had predicted another day of inclement weather. This had disheartened Susie, as the sat staring out of the window of the wooden, and unpainted four-room house, several yards from the muddy dirt road. Susie was in a state of misty blue. She wanted very much to go downtown to observe the dolls that had been featured in the display window of Mr. Johnson's Five-and-Dime Store.

"Susie, what ya lookin' at, gal? Ya ack like ya los' ya bes' frien'," Grandma Racheal warmly said.

"Nothing, Grandma," Susie replied.

"Gal, ya knows ya can't fool me. I've been 'round ya too long, and knows ya well."

"Nothing, really Grandma, honest.", Susie insisted.

"Well, if ya say so," Grandma Racheal said, returning to her rest.

Grandma Racheal had taken ill several months ago and had not recovered from the heart attack, leaving her confined to the beautifully designed oak bed that John had made. Susie stayed with her as much as she could between school and her chores. Susie always sat next to her grandmother's bed while doing her homework, as the lamp light and the fire in the fireplace reflected radiantly against the walls. Susie sometimes read stores to Grandma Racheal until she drifted silently to sleep.

The next day, Susie walked into the barn out back of the house where her Uncle John was busily carving out a chair for one of his customers. He was a well-known furniture maker in their neck of the woods. From the corner of his eyes, he noticed Susie sitting on the stool used for milking Sarah, the cow.

"What's the matta, Sue?", John asked compassionately, continuing at his work. Susie sat quietly for several seconds before she commenced to telling how much she wanted the doll that was displayed in the store window. When she had finished expressing her feelings, Susie was almost in tears. Uncle John calmly and affectionately said that money was scarce, and that her mother, Mrs. McCollum, would do her best for her and her siblings. Susie went away feeling better after the conversation.

The following day, Susie was able to share her feelings to Grandma Racheal, who had grown a little paler overnight. But she took the time to chat with Susie.

"Grandma, you okay?", Susie asked, concerned?

"Yes, chile, I be doin' alright," Grandma Racheal replied.

"Grandma, there's something I want for Christmas, but Ma might not be able to get it."

"What tis it, chile?", Grandma Racheal inquired.

"There's this doll in Mr. Johnson's store window that is so pretty! She's dressed in a pink dress with white lace at the collar, and at the hem a lovely white bow, and white booties, I want it, Grandma! I want it!", Susie blurted uncontrollably.

"Wait here, chile. I knows ya Ma will git ya what she can afford. Times is hard for everyone. But I'll yell ya this, ya pray and ast the Lord for it, He'll help you if He sees fit. The Lord knows all," were Grandma Racheal's final words before returning to her rest. Susie knew she could always talk with Grandma Racheal about almost anything. She was wise, patient, prudent, and kind with her words.

Christmas Eve, Susie and her siblings, Martha, Helen, John and Patrick, returned as normal children do, hoping Santa would be gracious with their requests. There was an accumulation of snow on the ground and the wind blew mildly, leaving a whisper as it ushered past the icy window. The stockings were hung over the fireplace as the flames forming the fire illuminated brightly, casting ghost-like shadows on the freshly papered walls. The cakes were baked and stored in the china closet for Santa's choosing. There were coconut, chocolates, vanillas, and two lucious fruit cakes. And one by one, the children fell asleep. Everything was ready for the coming of Christmas morning.

Mrs. McCollum sat next to Grandma Racheal's bed that night exhausted from her long day of delivering the supply of eggs and butter to her customers. She and Grandma Racheal sang several carols before sleep overtook both of them, with Mrs. McCollumn still seated in the rocking chair.

The next morning, just before dawn, the children were awakened to alarm. A painful and shattering scream was heard throughout the house. Sadly, Mrs. McCollumn awoke to discover that Grandma Racheal had passed away at some period during the night. The children hurried to the room to witness the shocking revelation. Susie became overwhelmed with grief. The tears fell uncontrollably. She had loved Grandma Racheal with all her heart. And now, the dearest person she had ever known was gone forever. The shock removed all semblance of Christmas.

"Children, there's nothing else we can do. Y'all go to the other room. If you want to, you can get your things from under the tree. We will take care of things here," Mrs. McCollum instructed.

At first Susie refused to leave the room. But when Mrs. McCollum gave her that confirming stare, Susie ran out of the room hysterically to the living room where she suddenly stood in frozen amazement and surprise. Sitting under the tree that had been lovingly adorned with many colorful ornaments was the doll she had fantasized over for months. Her tears of hurt and pain were instantly transformed into tears of joy. Susie picked up the doll and clung to it as though it meant her life.

Two days later, situated on a grassy hillside several feet from the small white church stood Susie, family and friends, next to Grandma Racheal's grave to say their final farewell. As the casket was lowered, Susie stood still with tear-filled eyes, unwilling and unwanting to say good-bye.

Though the years have come and gone, Susie remains hand length with a memorable past, while clinging to the blessed gift and her grandmother's cherished memory.

TRAVELER OF THE NIGHT

John McLeod left the warm secure confines of his home that sat deep within Gum Island that night about 9:15 p.m. He always had to walk the seven mile trip to his workplace at the Veneral Mill down the dark and desolate roads, especially the four mile stretch between Gunter's grocery and Drake, South Carolina.

Each side of the road was lined with thick forests that seemed to loom ghostly on the darkest of nights. It was one of the coldest nights of winter that John could remember since the three years of repetition, with the temperatures forecasted as being about nine degrees. But John knew he had no choice, due to the fact that he was and had been without an automobile for quite some time.

Each night he drudgedly left home and during the long and lonely walk to work, he thought about the wife and nine children he had left behind to provide for.

On many occasions John often contemplated his plight and the condition purgatory had placed on him.

John had made his exodus from city life and the exciting and comfortable amenities several years past where he had enjoyed some of the best of times. Now he found himself residing almost in the midst of the forest to care for his family on what seemed to be meager wages.

Draped in his long overcoat, a relic of World War II, John knew that even though times often seemed hard and foreboding, that his obligation dictated that no matter how audacious the task, that he must remain with his family-though he sometimes thought of leaving in search of finding better opportunity. But his love and devotion to his family eliminated any such possibility of that occurring.

On the night of December 24, 1963, something very unusual and mysterious happened. An occurrence that impounded on John's life and his family as long as his life remained.

John was fastly approaching his place of work next to the large Merchantile Store that had serviced numerous families during the heyday when cotton was king in Marlboro County; but, had lost its luster when many of the residents had migrated elsewhere. His steps were with great anticipation to escape from the dreadful cold, when suddenly and mysteriously a figure of a man dressed in black clothes stood several feet before him illuminated against the brightness of the light from the Merchantile.

Shocked and stunned, John stood deathlike, frozen in his step, unable to move or utter. By this time, he noticed that the figure that stood before him was faceless and lifeless with a hood that formed his head as though it was a shadow that stood like a man.

"Who you?", John asked with some hesitation?

The austere figure just remained there in its comotose state. At this time, John was about to make a flee, when a hollow voice was heard, penetrating the darkness saying, "I am the traveler of the Night. My name no man knows. I come as swiftly as the wind. I am that which cannot be seen. I am that which cannot be known. I am the mystery about which man wonders. I have walked with you on many occasions. Many nights, I have heard your thoughts, and felt your pain. I know you griefs, wishes, and have felt your desires. I understand the kind of life you envision for your family. I am here to offer you riches beyond the boundaries you have ever dreamed."

The words echoed in the corners of John's consciousness causing chills to reverberate his spine, and his heart to pound like the thunder of the worst storm he had ever witnessed.

Trembling with fear, John asked apprehensively, "Why me? What is it that I must do?"

"Simply walk with me," the sinister dark stranger instructed.

"I will be with you always, to guide your thoughts and decisions. Your family will enjoy their wishes and desires. They will want for nothing. I will become you, and you me."

"How is that?", John asked nervously.

From this night forward, my thoughts will be your thoughts, my decisions will be your decisions. For whatever I want, you will have," continued the stranger.

Suddenly the realization dawned upon John as to whom the mysterious shadow was, and the thought caused sweat to pop from the pores of his forehead as though he had just come out of a steamer. Momentarily, it appeared to John that he was running faster than he had ever run before. But, no matter how fast it seemed he was running, the figure continued to stand before him, until it became obvious to John that he never moved from the spot in which he stood.

Understanding John's decision, the frightful figure came forward with outstretched arms as if to embrace him when suddenly a bright and radiant light appeared amidst the clouds, as radiant as any light John had ever witnessed. With a blink of an eye, the cloaked and faceless stranger evaporated into a puff of smoke and John lept from his bed in hives of sweat, startling his wife almost out of her wits.

After regaining his composure, John removed himself from his bed, fell to his knees and began to pray. To thank God for all the goodness that his family had received over the years and to ask for God's continued blessing.

During the course of the following day, John shared in the joy that his family displayed. Thankful for the gifts they had received, and the love that showered from above.

A GLEAM OF HOPE

School had terminated the day before. Today was May 17, 1971, as I was awakened to the harmonious sounds of birds singing majestically in the old oak tree near my window. My! My head felt a little heavy after the graduation celebration of drinking and dancing the night before. Leaving high school is a major stepping-stone of life for everyone.

The sun had risen above the tree tops reflecting its rays through my window and casting shadows about my room. I lazily removed myself from the comfort of my bed and strolled to the window and let the shade up. I immediately felt my exhausted body rejuvenating from the warmth of the radiant sun, the fresh morning air and fragrance of the many types of vegetation which had begun to blossom as a result of spring.

Peering from my window, my mind wandered back in him to my childhood wherein I used to run and play in the huge yard surrounding our house. The various trees used to protect us from the scorching heat of summer. Though rest underneath the age old trees only lasted for a few minutes because of the time we spent working in the fields, it was blessing to our sweat-laden skin. During times of leisure, my brother Mark and had engineered our own golf course encircling the house. The clubs were made from oak limbs and the balls were hickory nuts from the trees. Each time we would play our games, it would last until the darkness had engulfed the sky.

"Charles, breakfast is ready," Mother called, intruding on my reminiscing.

"OK, I'll be there in a minute," I uttered back. I dressed hurriedly and headed to the table.

While eating, it dawned on me that I was supposed to call Paul a half hour ago to make certain that all supplies had been secured. During the past year, Paul, the gang and I had saved our hard earned cash to purchase supplies needed for our expedition. We had been comrades for the entire twelve years of our required education.

Ring -- ring!

"Hello," the soft mellow voice answered. It was Sharon, Paul's not-so-"little" sister. At age thirteen, she had turned the heads of many a young boy. It was though the gods had smiled and blessed her with the beauty and grace that would enlighten any male's heart.

"Hi, Sharon. Is Paul there?"

"Yes," she said seductively.

"Paul, it's Charles!", she said distantly.

"Hey, man, what's happening? Ready for our tedious journey?", Paul asked jokingly.

"Sure. Have you called the others?", I asked.

"Man, you're behind the times. The others have been called and are on their way to your house. See you in a few, sucker!", Paul exclaimed, hanging up the phone.

As I exited from the back door, I was greeted by our dog Rex. For a collie, he seemed overly exuberant this morning. He was a gift from my Uncle Marcus.

"Alright boy, I don't have time for you this morning. Have things to do." Totally ignored, Rex continued to jump up and down on my legs. Luckily for us both, a kitten passed by as though intimidating Rex into a chase. He ran after it, thus relieving me of having to become rude.

From where I was standing, I could see my dad and the others in the cucumber fields harvesting them for market. The land that produced the vegetation belonged to the McDonald family. We were sharecropping a third percentage. I sometimes hated the life we lived because of the hard work and little profit; but then, I also admired it because of the beauty and peacefulness of the surrounding.

Honk, honk!

Paul came speeding into the yard in his typical adroitness in driving. He was often referred to as the Richard Petty of rural dirt roads. Paul owned a blue and white Volkswagen van that his parents had purchased for him several months ago.

Prior to his arrival, I had checked my personal belongings that were stored in the shed out back of the house. Paul approached me dressed in his usual springs attire of shorts, sneakers and a T-Shirt.

"Everything ready?", I asked.

"Sure, ready as Freddy, brother. I'm ready for the woods," Paul enthusiastically implied.

"I thought you said the others were on the way over."

"I sure did! Maybe they stopped off somewhere. I don't know!"

Just as Paul made his statement, the gang arrived. They were all yelling and screaming with their arms and legs flying every which way on back of the pick-up truck Jerry was driving. He had borrowed it from his uncle Morris for the week of the outing.

Idell, the most provocative and sensual one of our group, seductively moved toward Paul. Putting her arms around his neck, she kissed him passionately. In reaction, Paul let go of a scream that brought mother storming out of the house in panic.

"What's wrong?", she insisted. Without a response except our laughing, she demanded to know what was going on.

"It's nothing, mother," I said, "Just a practical joke."

"Please, for God's sake, don't scare me like that again," Mother responded.

After a few minutes, the laughter had ceased and we mapped out our strategy for the adventure ahead. Within an hour we were on our way. Our first stop would be at Hunter's Grocery Store off Highway 38.

During my younger years, I remember vividly on many occasions walking with my brother Mark, the Wilson and Brunton boys that several miles to Hunter's. There were times when we knew he had cheated us but, because of times racially, we momentarily relinquished our rights. Though we felt he knew he was taking advantage of us due to color and age, he never got away scot free. On the days we would go there to sell old bottles to him we would, after emptying the sacks, place all of the sacks in the bottom of one. This would muffle the sound of the ice cream, cakes and other goodies that we discreetly and politely had dropped in.

When arriving at the store, we spotted Mr. Hunter standing in his usual posture in the doorway with his hand propped against the door post. He was a slender man who wore his hair in a crew cut. He was extremely pale due to a kidney disorder.

"Good morning," we all voiced in union as we approached the doorway.

"Morning. What y' all up to?", he asked inquisitively.

"We're going on a hiking trip!", Pamela retorted.

"Where to?", he asked.

"Gum Island!", Paul exclaimed.

"Y' all know that place is dangerous, don't cha?", Mr. Hunter warned.

Inside the store Paul continued boastfully, "Who's afraid of danger? Danger is my nickname. I can take care of any situation that might arise!"

"Don't say I didn't warn ya," Mr. Hunter replied while making his way behind the counter.

"We'll be alright," I said assuredly. "It'll only be for a week."

Each of us purchased some ice cream. We then started for Blenheim, which was our final stop before reaching Dunbar.

The ride to Blenheim was 3-1/2 miles. During the short ride we continued to make our plans and assign each person's responsibilities. We were stopping at the famous Blenheim Ale Distributing plant to purchase an assortment of soft drinks.

Upon arrival, I noticed that there were several out of state cars parked down the road at the spring. Travelers were always stopping at the spring to sample the fresh mineral water. It was rumored that the spring was discovered by a Civil War foot soldier. When he accidentally stepped into a hole and pulled his leg free, the water purged forth and has continued to flow until this day!

The ride to Dunbar, where we would abandon the convenience of the truck and the van, conveyed a most beautiful scenic view. The greenery displayed was much for the eye to behold. The sun was not yet stationed in mid-sky. There was an occasional cloud in the distance and the cotton had grown several inches from the ground outlining a panoramic view as far as the eye could see. At a distance you could also see the waves of heat swarming across the fields like the cresting of water across the ocean. Further down the road, there were rows of tobacco plants that had grown about two feet in height. Across the field near the edge of the woods, there was a man sitting on a tractor resting from the toil and heat of the morning sun.

Just before reaching Dunbar, we passed a stretch of road that illuminated a shadowy path that emulated from a thicket of trees. Some of those limbs extended nearly half way across the road from each side almost connecting. It reminded me of my desire and how much I was looking forward to challenging the forest that had claimed so many lives.

Once there was a trio of hunters who had gotten lost for a period of two weeks before two of them were found alive. The other one had succumbed to pneumonia on the eighth day. On another occasion in 1964, a couple of soldiers who had parachuted into the swamp were killed when they were bitten by rattlesnakes. We now know they were on maneuvers preparing for the war in Viet Nam. From the outside a beauty exuded that was enticing to the imagination but within was an evil that dared all who attempted to challenge it.

Our adventure would begin in the wooded area near the small town of Dunbar with a population of about one hundred. We had made arrangements with Pam's uncle, Mr. Simpson, to leave the vehicles at his place until we returned.

"Good morning, Uncle Simpson. Where's Aunt Mollie?", Pamela asked.

"Hello chillin! Mama's out back foolin' around wit dem chickens. Y'all know how she jus' loves dem dar chicks."

The couple, though they had never told their ages, had to be in their mid-eighties. Mrs. Simpson was one of the nicest, sweetest ladies you could ever want to meet and know. The community's most beloved citizen. It was a rare occasion that whenever we visited that she didn't have some of her homemade treats for us. Her manner of dress reminded me of my grandmother with the bonnet on her head, a dress that reached to her ankles and those thick, beige support hose. The typical attire for most of the older women in these parts. Mr. Simpson attired himself in the usual blue jeans, plaid shirt and low topped tan boots. Except for Sundays or an occasional Saturday, this is what you found the inhabitants of Dunbar wearing.

Mr. Simpson was constantly teasing Mrs. Simpson about one thing or another. She would always pretend to be displeased. They had been married for almost sixty years and as Mrs. Simpson often said, "We love each other more as each day passes."

We filled our canteens and our five-gallon thermos with water from their pump, said our goodbyes and promised the Simpsons that we would be careful. We walked around the edge of the woods for about a mile before actually entering the forest. Once we had entered and reached the first clearing, we stopped to decide who would lead and who would take protectionary measures.

James' familarity with the out-of-doors made him a unanimous choice for the lead position. "Sampson" Joe Young would take up the rear and because of his bold nature, Victor would act as scout. Five minutes elapsed in the process of organizing positions. Finally we had begun our expedition in earnest!

The going was relatively easy at first but, after an hour, we began to encounter some difficulty. The thickets and vines became extremely dense and required a lot of chopping with our machetes. Idell had begun to tire from her "assumed" work effort. We all knew she wouldn't be much help with the heavy work but, as an added source of fun, delight and a friend, we invited her to come along.

Hours passed before we decided to take a break. It was four o'clock in the evening. Though we were tired, everyone began to rehash old jokes that had been told year after year. George, better known as Mr. Genius, just sat and listened. He never joined in our silliness and usually laughed at jokes no one else thought funny. He was excellent at subjects that had some intellectual relevance or when a debate arose.

At four thirty we commenced onward. The surroundings had become immensely crowded with brush requiring added effort on our parts. Derrick's asthmatic condition began to take its toll on him. Fortunately it was getting close to seven o'clock,

100

the time we had agreed to make camp. Victor had gone on ahead to secure a suitable place free of brush.

"Ok, this is it, gang. We'll call it a day," I said. An hour transpired before the tents were prepared. The sun had almost disappeared from the sky and old night had begun to creep upon us. The camp was set up in a semi-circle similar to the way the pioneers used to set up wagon trains in the old west. A couple of rifles and a shotgun had been brought along to protect us from whatever evils might befall us.

Upon completion of a meal of pork-n-beans and sausage, we sat around the fire reminiscing about our years of school and projecting what our futures would be. Idell, as though it was a secret, confessed that she wanted to become a model and possibly an actress. Standing and posing for her "audience", she exhibited a figure that would take the breath away from the most virile of men.

"I'm planning to acquire my Ph.D. in Psychology, with perhaps a Master's in Sociology," George interjected. "I want to be in a position to help those who may have problems adjusting to the difficult and complex occurrences of society," he concluded. He was always direct and brief.

"Well, I'm going to join the Air Force and travel around the world. I hope to pursue a career in electronics. Maybe I'll return home one day to set up my own business," Billy explained. "I think it is important that someone return to the community to help create some of the changes that are needed."

"Man, you're crazy! I don't think I'll ever come back to this place after I leave. These people are afraid of progress and when you try to do something that's positive, they jump down throat. No! I'll never come back," Paul cried angrily. He had always had difficulty in expressing his feelings calmly. His mother had often cautioned him about getting upset over things that he couldn't readily change or control. "People have their ways, Paul, and time has a way of correcting things," she would advise him.

In many ways I sympathized with Paul's feelings. There wasn't much opportunity available in the area, especially if you were Black. Ironically and potent, if you were Black and from the wrong side of the fence. I reluctantly confirmed that I had not made any plans for the future. My family needed me to help complete the harvest, after which I would try to get a job at one of the local textile mills.

"I doubt if I'll come back once I leave. I've been thinking about making a career in the Marines. You know, where they build men, but only a chosen few. Anyway, my mother needs money to help support the family. This'll be one way that I could contribute financially," Sampson continued.

George asked Pamela what her plans were. She replied, "For one thing. I won't be leaving. I plan to take up nursing at Marlboro Technical College, I'll get a job at the hospital, get married and live a simple life with the man I love," she warmly said.

Tommy and Helen's plans were similar. They both were going to attend South Carolina State College. Tommy was considering a major in Business Administration, and Helen's was Elementary Education. Victor had received a scholarship in football from Johnson C. Smith University.

Before retiring for bed, we sat around the translucent campfire enjoying the surrounding beauty and listening to the familiar sounds of the crickets chirping in the distance. Far away we could hear the barking of dogs presumably tracking some woodland creature. As the echoes penetrated the brisk air, I thought I heard something creeping in the nearby bushes. After listening intently, I realized it was just my imagination.

For the next couple of days we followed the course of our plans almost mechanically. The going became more tedious as we delved deeper into the forest.

On the fourth morning about six thirty, the girls had completed their responsibilities of preparing the food. A typical menu of grits, eggs, bacon and bread for those who preferred it. At seven thirty we were traveling once again. Victor had left earlier, leaving a visible trail. Though it still required quite a bit of cutting for a cleared passage, it was exhilirating to be out trailblazing with friends you grew up with.

Thirty minutes later Victor came running back towards us sweating and frantic. Almost too exhausted to speak, he tried desperately to alert us of his discovery. Everyone tried to calm him down as best they could but he was out of it. Finally he came to himself enough to explain his panic.

A distance further up the makeshift path, lying next to a small log, was a skeleton of a human being! We accompanied Victor to the location and found a deteriorated hat, scraps of clothing and a pair of boots. We moved closer to inspect the remains. Sampson, in his courageous demeanor, bent down and touched the skeleton whereupon it fell over onto the ground.

"Who do you think it is?", Idell nervously asked.

"I don't know, Maybe it was someone who got lost or something," Tommy said,

"No. If it was someone who had gotten lost, we would have heard of it," Paul explained.

"What are we going to do about it?", George asked.

"Report it to the Sheriff," exclaimed Helen, "I think it's the best thing we can do."

"But what about our adventure?," cried Idell. "We've come too far to turn back now!"

"Don't be so selfish, Idell," I snapped. "We must report this to the authorities. We're only on our fourth day. It would be foolish not to report it as soon as possible."

"I think that one or two of us should return to Simpson's and alert the police to our find," said George. "It's the decent and right thing to do."

"I'll go," said Victor. "We've made a trail and it'll be easy to go back. You guys make camp here and wait."

Off he went. I knew that with his stamina he was the choice for the journey back. Victor prided himself on his physical ability. He had been named the M.V.P. as the number one running back in the Conference and also the state. Rushing for over 1800 yards for two consecutive years made me feel secure that he would prevail.

While sitting against a huge pine tree resting, it dawned on me that a hunter had been reported missing about three years ago. To my knowledge he had not been found. I looked over at the remains and thought, what a dreadful way to die, desolate from the world he had known!

103

For the remainder of the day we engaged in general conversation. After we had eaten, set up and camp and secured our supplies, we resumed our conversation which centered on our discovery. We talked about the fate of the corpse and if Victor was making it alright. We had given him a rifle for protection.

Soon night was upon us. It was bedtime. We each made our way to our tents. We exchanged good nights all around. As I was about to enter my tent, there came this sharp, piercing scream that cut through the dark night like a hot knife through butter! It came from the area of Idell and Helen's tent. A second later Helen came racing from the tent as though she had encountered the devil himself.

"It's Idell," she blurted hysterically with tears streaming down her face. "She-she-she fell on a snake!"

We dashed to the tent and carefully pulled it open. Astonishingly, there lying next to Idell was a rattler as big as any I had ever seen curled in its defensive position, ready to strike. Unfortunately it was plain to see that it had aready bitten Idell. Sampson quickly retrieved one of the rifles and proceeded to repeatedly shoot the thing. Assured that the snake had met its demise, we quickly pulled Idell from the tent. Apparently she had been bitten several times in her upper body, due to the swelling in that area. She had begun to sweat profusely and started to convulse violently.

"Get the medical kit!", I screamed, pushing George in the direction of the kit.

Within seconds he returned but there was little in the kit to help save Idell. Idell began to scream and wrench as though crazed. All we could do was sit and watch and cry. Her situation was hopeless. About twenty minutes later Idell drew her last breath. It seemed at that moment something reached inside of me and attempted to rip my insides out. I knew from looking at the others that they felt a similar pain. For a couple of hours we just sat huddled together, continuing to sulk in agony and pain. Helen had been reduced to a state of shock and nothing we did would bring her around.

After we had composed ourselves, us guys gathered together to explore our options. Upon pain-wrenching deliberation, it was decided that we would start back at daybreak. We felt that Victor should be a day and a half from the Simpsons and this would lessen the time and distance of being found. We would only carry the bare necessities because we would be taking turns pulling Idell's body on a stretcher that we had spent most of the night preparing.

As I lay there in the remaining hours of the night, it was difficult and almost impossible to comprehend the position purgatory had placed on us. Amidst us lay two corpses, that of a stranger and someone we had clearly loved and admired. My eyes began to moisten with the unused tears of grief. They uncontrollably streamed down my face as I remembered a friend.

I leaped to my feet with the touch of something fumbling at my shoulder. It was Mark alerting me to the fact that it was six thirty and time to begin our troublesome journey. Apparently the others had been up for a while because they had already eaten; they were ready for travel. I quickly ate my meal and helped the fellows bury and mark the skeleton that we had found. We left.

Sampson took the first turn at pulling the stretcher. The trip returning was much easier thanks to our makeshift trail. The pace was slower because Helen was still in a state of limbo and had to be assisted.

Travel was constant until ten a.m. We knew we would have to make as much time as possible until we were found. By the time we rested everyone was almost exhausted. I just wanted to sleep and remain there for several hours. Suddenly my mind began to wander and reflect on what good times we shared with Idell. She was always so full of life and gaiety. If you wanted a party fired up, she was the one to call. She had won several area beauty contests and pageants. She had just been crowned our school's Homecoming Queen this past fall. Even though most of the girls thought of her as a flirt, only those of us who knew her well knew that it was just a façade. Idell deeply cared about others and their feelings. Her perspectives on life transcended beyond the childish notions of today.

For added comfort and to stay in touch with the outside world, we had brought along a portable radio. Tommy abruptly made a suggestion that we utilize it every so often to determine if Victor had made it back and if there was any word on our plight. We had it turned on for only a few minutes when WBSC announced that a severe storm was headed our way accompanied by high winds and possibly hail. There was also a tornado watch out for the area.

"You heard that?", George asked, as if his ears were the only ones tuned in.

"Yeah, man, you think we're deaf or something?", Paul stammered, annoyed.

"What's your problem? I was only asking," George snapped back.

"Ok, let's not argue guys. We have enough problems as it is. Let's keep cool," I said.

"I think we had better make some times and tracks," Mark retorted.

"You're right!", Tommy exclaimed, jumping to his feet.

Clouds had begun to form to the north of us. Though no one verbalized it, the tension and anxiousness had started to mount. The pace had increased and there was no mention of a break from anyone for 2-1/2 hours of travel. The clouds were cast overhead. An assortment of charcoal gray, dark blue, black and white cottony clouds provided a a roof over us. The wind had increased by several knots and caused the limbs of the trees to bear down and brush our faces.

Fear began to grip at my every nerve as I'm sure it did the others. The sky soon became as dark as night. The lightening was so bright that it was like a lamp flashing on and off. The thunder was so loud that it seemed as though the ground was vibrating. It was time we found shelter as best we could. By this time the storm was striking at us full force. Time for everyone to look out for themselves.

George took Helen and led her behind a large, sturdy oak tree. Moments later the rain began to pour as if from buckets. Looking about to the best of my ability, I could see that everyone was using parts of the tents for protection. Limbs commenced to crack and fall, some of them close to where I was crouched. Every once in a while someone called out and a chain reaction was initiated to confirm that everyone was alright.

Night had fallen and the rain continued to come down in torrents and the wind continued to blow. Once more we made our roll call. All present and accounted for. About ten p.m. the rain and wind let up enough for us to crawl out from under our shelters. After conversing for a few minutes, we decided to try to travel at night. Good suggestion, I thought; but it was going to be rough considering the fallen debris and the fact that night was upon us. We all knew that we must make time because even though the storm had subsided, it was far from being over.

The major obstacle we now faced was whether to continue to carry Idell's body. The difficult decision was made to bury her there and mark the grave. Helen was taken away by George and not allowed to know our plans. As we carried out our grief stricken plan, an emptiness engulfed me like I had never known before. The feelings from the night before came so strongly that I was blinded to my surroundings. MY FRIEND IDELL! I cried within for the waste of it all.

One o'clock, and we had made considerable progress. Though it wasn't certain that we were on the right path, we were at least getting closer to the Simpsons. Soaked and miserable, we pushed on until it was five o'clock a.m. Mark had come down with a fever causing our situation to go from worse to almost impossible.

"I sure wish I was back at home," George said sincerely.

"I wish we were all back home, " Tommy responded agitated.

"I hope the storm is over," Mark said,

"I wonder how far we've come," Sampson asked.

"I don't know," I said, "but I hope that we've traveled half the distance home," knowing all the time hadn't covered much ground.

We tried getting reception on the radio but all we got was static. Apparently something had happened to the station. Our food supply was getting low; we only had enough to last one more day. We ate half of our rations and decided to rest where we were.

After about an hour of travel the next day, a familiar sight was seen. The canal that we had crossed came into view. We were only a day and a half away. Certainly Victor should have made it home by now, I thought. The canal was only a few yards away, but it seemed as though it would take forever to reach it.

"Let's try the radio again!" Tommy exclaimed, reaching inside his bag. Only static.

About the time we were about to cross the logs of the canal, the sky abruptly commenced to darken again. Simultaneously the horn at the fire tower between Bingham and Dunbar began to alarm. Suddenly the wind started to blow violently. The sound of several freight trains colliding came to my ears. Looking around terrified, I realized that the trees had begun to collapse all around us. Though the canal was half filled with water, in order to survive, we would have to find shelter within it. IN addition to the threatening tornado and the water, we would have to contend with and be careful of the moccasins that had been known to nest in the canal.

As we lay in the murky water scared out of our wits, trees were uprooted and fell in the canal all around us. "Help, help!", resounded the screams of one of our female travel companions. A tree branch had fallen mid-way across Sampson, submerging him under water. For the next few moments, we worked desperately to release him. Several minutes later and he was free! There were no apparent injuries and we continued to huddle together drawing strength from each other. As quickly as it came, the wind ceased; the rain continued to pour steadily. The remaining supplies were scattered in the water. The rain kept coming in torrents. We had removed ourselves to the other side of the canal and hibernated amidst some fallen trees. By now I knew that we were being searched for.

We were able to salvage some of the food. Only the canned goods. Helen was still very depressed. Mark's pneumonia was getting worse. We were all suffering from the dampness. Periodically chills would overtake me but I would not let it be noticeable to the others.

"I hope the weather clears up tomorrow," Sampson said.

"I do, too." Tommy responded.

"I know our families are worried out of their minds," reflected George.

"I sure hope tomorrow is our lucky day." Tommy said between coughs.

Day broke and we were on our way, moving at a steady pace with the anticipation of being found, or at least arriving safely at the Simpsons. The sky was beginning to clear. Visibility was better. We soon realized we were off course but that didn't matter as long as our compass indicated we were headed north by northwest. With every step I could only think about home and the secure confines within. Boy, it sure would be great to see all of those smiling faces and to hear all of those talkative mouths.

Around the house there was always plenty of action. Never a dull moment. It was a constant battle for mother to try and keep everyone in line. To add to her frustrations, on Sundays the whole neighborhood of kids would come over our way. Most had to walk a half mile but it was worth it to enjoy those few hours for they were few and far in between.

We had come upon a thicket area where the wind had not caused much damage. From the looks of things, we were way off course. Even if Victor had made it, and there was a search going on, our location couldn't easily be identified.

"Man, I thought we were almost home," Tommy exclaimed. "And we are as lost as ever. What are we going to do now?"

"We will just have to continue," I said, trying to convince everyone that we would make it out of this predicament soon.

From the looks of things, the tornado had gone in one straight path. Now the forest was thick as when we first began our expedition. Sampson and I had to do most of the cutting to clear a path that was easier to follow. The work was tedious and demanding but, at this time, I was bent on doing whatever was necessary to get the hell out of there. It was late evening before we finally took a break. Suddenly we heard a plane coming our way. Quickly the thought occurred that it may be on a search mission! With all the growth round us, it would be tremendously difficult for them to detect us. We had to act quickly! We began waving frantically at the plane as it flew overhead and took another turn and came again in our direction. We would have to alert them to our location as soon as possible. If not, we would probably have to remain another night in what had become a living hell!!

The sun wasn't long for the sky. It occurred to me that Helen still clung to Idell's makeup kit. There should certainly be a mirror in it, I thought. I grabbed the bag in desperation and frantically searched for a mirror. The plane was approaching at a rapid speed. Upon finding the much sought after object, I found a section clear enough to trap a beam of sunlight on the mirror. I held it so that it would gleam towards the plane's path. The plane flew over once again and I continued to hold the mirror while the others yelled and screamed.

The plane gone and the sun had faded below the tree tops. Subdued and exhausted, we retired for the night. All of our food was gone but we had an ample supply of water, thanks to the torrential rains. Sleep didn't come easy for anyone. As we sat about, no one spoke. Each one caught up in their own thoughts. One by one we dropped off to sleep.

Awakened the next morning by various animal sounds nearby, I was heavy laden to discover that a dense fog had crept in overnight. It was almost impossible to see your hand in front of your face. It didn't take long to figure out that there would be another delay. We sat around and engaged in meaningless conversation to pass the time away.

About 10:30 there was a little visibility and we began to move anxiously to end our ordeal. We headed in the direction we thought to be towards home. We hadn't gone five feet when suddenly we heard the sound of dogs barking! It was the sound of bloodhounds coming our way. We just stood there and listened until we heard the sound of voices calling our names. Sampson sprinted in the direction the voices, leaving us behind. Shortly he returned with the search party which included most of our fathers. At that moment I thought of Idell as I saw her father enter the clearing.

We cried and held on to each other for what seemed like an eternity. Finally we were ushered off in the direction we knew to be home, in safety and in the care of those who loved us.